WALKS WITH CHILDREN
IN THE
SURREY HILLS

Other Questa Guides, published and
in production

Walks with Children in the Lake District:
Buttermere and the Vale of Lorton
Borrowdale
Patterdale
Around Coniston

Walks with Children in the Yorkshire Dales:
Swaledale and Wensleydale

Kielder Country Walks
Brontë Country Walks

WALKS with CHILDREN
in the
SURREY HILLS

ANDREW McCLOY

A Questa Guide

© Andrew McCloy 1995
ISBN 1 898808 08 2
Maps by Benedict Davies

Questa Publishing
27 Camwood, Clayton Green, Bamber Bridge
PRESTON, Lancashire, PR5 8LA

ADVICE TO READERS

Readers are advised that while the author has taken
every effort to ensure the accuracy of this guidebook,
and has been required to revisit all the routes during the
course of preparing the book, changes can occur which
may affect the contents. The publishers would welcome
notes of any changes that they find.
This guidebook has been compiled in accordance with
the *Guidelines for Writers of Path Guides* published by
the Outdoor Writers' Guild.

Also by Andrew McCloy
Land's End to John o'Groats

Printed by
Carnmor Print and Design, London Road, Preston

CONTENTS

KEY TO MAPS

The maps in this book are produced at two scales. One is 1:25000, the other, 1:17500. Distances on these maps are represented as follows:

1:25000 (Walks 1, 2, 3, 4, 5, 6, 7, 8, 9, 11, 13)

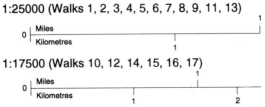

1:17500 (Walks 10, 12, 14, 15, 16, 17)

The following symbols have been used on all maps:

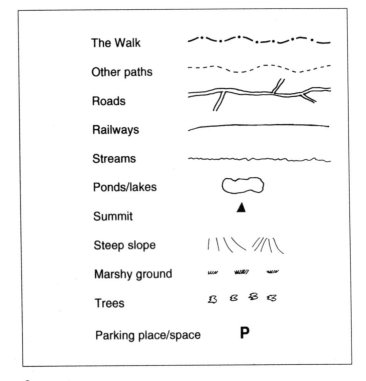

The Walk	
Other paths	
Roads	
Railways	
Streams	
Ponds/lakes	
Summit	
Steep slope	
Marshy ground	
Trees	
Parking place/space	P

THE SURREY HILLS

For a county often dismissed as London's back garden, Surrey has a lot to offer the walker, from sweeping chalk downs to thick, wooded hills; open commons and beautiful, mixed woodland to some of the most important heathland left in southern England. There are miles of inviting public footpaths and bridleways, several long distance footpaths, including a National Trail, country parks and local nature trails, and of course Leith Hill, the highest point in the South East.

Above all, Surrey is user-friendly. I have early memories of romping around Box Hill, Ranmore and Holmbury, with the wide, grassy slopes and undulating woodland tracks providing hours of safe and enjoyable exploration. People of all ages and abilities wander these paths and spaces as much today, and for many families tied to the congested, urban centres of the South East, Surrey's green and gentle miles are, quite literally, a breath of fresh air.

The 17 walks in this book cover not just the tree-topped greensand ridges centred on Leith Hill and Holmbury Hill, but also the sandy heaths south west of Guildford, plus the imposing crests of the North Downs, with its open slopes and dramatic viewpoints. For such a small county Surrey has tremendous variety, and a surprisingly green covering - the panorama revealed from the famous viewpoint at the top of Box Hill confirms the fact that Surrey has one of the most rich and extensive canopies of trees of any county in England. And this splendid variety of scenery means that every member of the family is catered for, whether your interest is in butterflies, windmills, geology, old churches, wild flowers, industrial archaeology or tea rooms.

From a geological point of view, Surrey's dominant high ground is of course the North Downs which, like its attractive sister in Sussex, provides a firm, green barrier across the county, and actually extends as far east as the Kent coast. The gentle northern slopes of the Downs gradually dip to the London Clays underpinning the capital; while south of the chalk are the narrow greensand ridges that include the county's high-spot, Leith Hill. Beyond this the Wealden sands and clays form a lower

7

landscape of heath and forest that extends into Sussex.

The ancient forest of the Weald, in fact, was responsible for one of the few major industries in the area. The lack of any important mineral deposits and relatively few waterways, plus the generally poor, thin soils which discouraged intensive agricultural development, meant that settlement in the county had been relatively light. But in the sixteenth and seventeenth centuries an iron industry grew up that used the Weald's rich woodland to make charcoal for smelting. Although this was short-lived, other pockets of industry included the small but important Chilworth gunpowder mills on the Tilling Bourne river (see Walk 12). The transport revolution, however, brought Surrey into the commuter belt for the fast-expanding capital, and local centres such as Reigate, Dorking and Guildford became more accessible for London's affluent workforce. Green Belt measures had to be introduced to safeguard London's rural boundaries; but despite this, mechanical diggers are widening the M25 at Reigate Hill as I write, and another precious piece of Surrey is being lost.

With so much chalk and sandy ground prevailing, Surrey's paths drain fairly well and most of the time mud is only a problem immediately after rain or where mountain bikes and horses proliferate. Even so, stout footwear is recommended for the walks involving considerable height gain and longer distances, since walking shoes and boots will offer greater ankle protection and will be much more comfortable in the long run. And, on another practical note, make sure that you take a daysack containing not just a map and waterproofs but also extra food and drink, since not all of Surrey's villages have refreshment points, and shops are often closed on Sundays.

The waymarking of Surrey's public footpaths is generally quite good, but if a signpost is missing or a stile is broken then make sure you report it to the Highways and Transportation Department at Surrey County Council.

Many of the walks described in this book are accessible by public transport, and where appropriate bus and train details are given. For more information on routes and timetables, plus a handy public transport map of the county, call Surrey County Council's public transport enquiry line on 01737 223000. Try leaving the car behind and have a stress-free day out in the countryside!

WALK 1:
BOX HILL

After a few minutes savouring the fine views
southwards, this route leaves the escarpment for
woodland, then wanders down the bottom of a
secluded chalk valley, rich in wildlife.
To leave it requires an initially steep climb among
trees, then flat and easy forest tracks to the café
and visitor centre.

Start: National Trust car park, top of Box Hill. GR.179514.
Bus Route 16 (Epsom-Dorking).
Maps: OS Landranger 187/Pathfinder 1206.
Total distance: 5km (3 miles).
Height gain: 100m (340 feet).
Difficulty: A short and mostly easy walk, but with one steep ascent that
could be difficult if the ground is wet.

THE WALK:

From the popular trig point on the top of Box Hill walk east (towards Reigate) along the North Downs Way (indicated by white acorn signs). Soon this level track enters trees, and where it crosses a sunken lane turn left and take this former coach road from Dorking the few paces up to the car park of Boxhills, a pub/café. Cross the road and join the clearly-marked bridleway, a wide, firm track that heads into thick woodland. Where it meets three others, continue straight on, indicated by a finger post, and down the gradually-sloping valley.

As you progress down Juniper Bottom the trees thin out, and the chalk valley becomes more and more interesting. The massive yew tree on the right is thought to be over 250 years old; and further on there is a handsome stand of larch and Norwegian spruce.

Finally, turn off left on to a

public footpath up the wooded hillside (opposite a stile, and before a hedged-off field opens up on the left). This path is clear and unmissable, but to begin with it is steep and should be the main track maintains a fairly direct but now more gentle route over the wooded flank of Lodge Hill. For a while this path runs along the top of open downland above Box Hill's famous Zig Zag

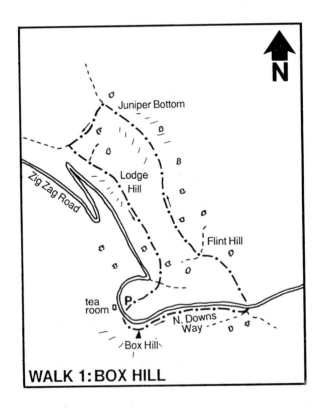

WALK 1: BOX HILL

taken slowly. Gradually it eases, and where it meets a broader forest track turn left on to this and continue uphill.

Ignore paths off to the left, as

Road. The meadows below support a range of flowers and insects, including many species of moths and butterflies.

Once back in the mixed

plantation the straight, wide track is easy to follow. Pass a small clearing of mature beech trees on your left, and soon afterwards the path emerges close to the National Trust café and visitor centre.

POINTS OF INTEREST

Box Hill Country Park: This popular and scenic location attracts many visitors simply because of the superlative views: Chanctonbury Ring on the South Downs is visible on a clear day (24 miles away), while nearer at hand you can watch the aircraft taking off at Gatwick (8 miles) and study the wooded greensand hills beyond Dorking. Below the steep, grassy slopes of Box Hill, where the underlying chalk is often noticeable, the River Mole snakes its way through a gap in the North Downs towards the Thames.

As to the hill's name, the dense evergreen box tree (which produces a hard wood favoured by engravers) was cultivated on these slopes up until the last century. Although some box scrub remains, the carefully-managed plantations now generally contain beech, oak and cherry, plus a mix of coniferous (evergreen) trees, such as pine, maple and spruce.

Near the car park and main viewpoint there is an educational National Trust centre, which includes a working bee hive. The buildings are known as Fort Cottages, and are named after a former fortification and ammunition dump that was built here in the late 1800s. In the woods behind is a stone which purports to mark the grave of a local eccentric, Major Peter Labelliere, who - by his own request - was buried vertically, head first. Further down the path the trees give way to a long and lovely (and safe) grass meadow that slopes down invitingly to the Burford Bridge Hotel in the Mole valley.

This is a great place for a picnic in the afternoon sunshine. Dorking, spread out far below, resembles a giant toytown, with what appears to be miniature trains and cars going about their business. These slopes are also popular with skiers in winter. However, the climb back up can be VERY arduous for legs of all ages.

WALK 2:
RANMORE COMMON

This walk encircles the National Trust's Ranmore Common, and begins and ends with an easy stroll through glorious mixed woodland that is well-known for its springtime bluebells. In between there are views of the Trust's famous house, Polesden Lacey, and a visit to the ancient Tanner's Hatch Youth Hostel.

Start: National Trust car park, Ranmore Common Road. GR.142504. Dorking Station one mile.
Maps: OS Landranger 187/Pathfinder 1206.
Total distance: 5km (3 miles).
Height gain: 115m (375 feet).
Difficulty: Easy.

THE WALK:

From the car park head west along the roadside track for a few yards, then immediately after Fox Cottages take the left of two public footpaths into the trees. The beautiful mixed woodland includes beech, oak and yew, and simply brims with wildlife. The path is obvious, and after crossing another descends to a small valley bottom where you should turn right on to a clear bridleway.

Continue amid bushes and trees that sport berries of many types: elderberry, blackberry and buckthorn (large black berries) are all present, but don't try eating anything unless you are sure that they are safe. As you near the edge of the wood there are views across fields of Polesden Lacey, a restored Regency villa now owned by the National Trust and open to the public. Its 60 acres of grounds include theme gardens, sculptured lawns and open-air theatre in the summer.

The winding track soon passes Tanner's Hatch Youth

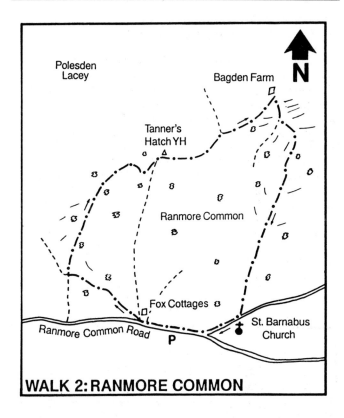

Polesden Lacey

Bagden Farm

N

Tanner's Hatch YH

Ranmore Common

Fox Cottages

St. Barnabus Church

Ranmore Common Road

P

WALK 2: RANMORE COMMON

Hostel. Originally built in 1642 as two cottages and restored earlier this century, it remains a simple and basic establishment, with no electricity or telephone. It has a lovely, secluded setting, and there is a small adventure playground outside. (The hostel also has a 4-bed room available for families.)

Continue down the lane past the hostel, and where it curves left by fields take a gated bridleway to the right and follow the rough track through the middle of a wide, green field via a large oak tree. At Bagden Farm turn right for a fenced bridleway uphill, soon forking left up a short but mildly steep gravelly track. Behind there are splendid views along the dry chalk valley towards Tanner's Hatch.

Into the woods once more, and soon the wide and direct track evens out and eventually emerges opposite the flint-decorated St Barnabus Church. It styles itself "the Church on the North Downs Way". Turn right and follow the lane or its wide verge (which is indeed the course of the North Downs Way) back to Ranmore Common Road and to the car park.

Should you still hanker more views or a picnic site, then Denbies Hillside, behind the car park, is well worth exploring, and an information board has details of a short nature trail.

ALONG THE WAY:

Butterflies: The chalk downland of places such as Ranmore Common, Box Hill (Walk 1) and Mickleham Downs (Walk 5) support a large butterfly population. Blue-coloured butterflies are particularly prevalent. Look out for the adonis and chalk-hill, and later in the year the silver-spotted skipper. Others include the orange tip (with distinctive orange tipped white wings), brimstone (yellow), and many of the copper family.

Winkworth Arboretum

In 1937 Dr Wilfrid Fox began planting Winkworth Arboretum (an arboretum is simply a place where many different kinds of trees and shrubs are grown). He introduced many exotic varieties, and - especially in the spring and autumn - the colours of the maples, azaleas and cherries are spectacular. The grounds are large and varied, with a maze of paths and tracks. There are gardens, bluebell and holly woods, an alpine meadow, and two scenic lakes (the far bank of the large one has a wide, grassy picnic area).

WALK 3:
WINKWORTH ARBORETUM

The route begins with a brief tour of the National Trust's Winkworth Arboretum (there is a small entry charge), although the wooded parkland and lakes are worth a whole afternoon's exploration on their own; then it takes to the quiet hills opposite. The marvellous views are ever-changing and extensive. After this the Greensand Way leads through a quiet, wooded valley, then crosses another, before returning to the car park from the south.

Start: Winkworth Arboretum main car park, off B2130. GR.989413.
Bus Routes 44, 46 (Guildford-Cranleigh).
Maps: OS Landranger 186/Pathfinders 1225 and 1226.
Total distance: 8km (5 miles).
Height gain: 190m (625 feet).
Difficulty: Moderate. Although short and relatively low, there are several quite steep climbs, plus a couple of high stiles.

THE WALK:

Enter the Arboretum by the main entrance, where there are tearooms and toilets, and proceed down the path to Rowes Flashe Lake below. From the boathouse take the track north to Phillimore Lake, smaller and more overgrown. The path curves around the far end, with fields on the left, and just after Phillimore Cottage take an easily overlooked but way-marked footpath to the left. This traverses several fields (watch out for a small patch of nettles between two stiles) then turns right over a stile by a gate and down to a metalled lane. Turn right, then soon left at a T-junction, in Thorncombe Street. Almost immediately turn right, up a narrowing lane by a cottage with white posts on the verge outside.

This lovely overgrown lane turns into a path between rough hedges, but is quite steep. Soon sweet chestnut trees, then over yet another stile and through a small area of bracken and young trees before emerging at the top of a long, wide field. The views east are to Holmbury

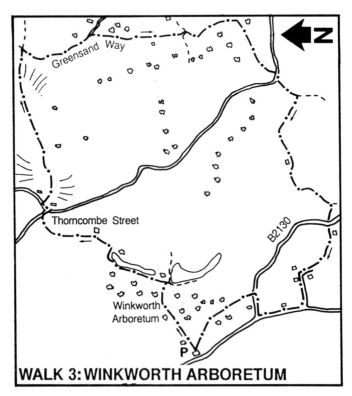

WALK 3: WINKWORTH ARBORETUM

there are glorious views up and down the pleasing, part-forested valley. At the top of the slope carry on over a stile and through a field to another stile. Now walk beneath some large Hill, Leith Hill and Hurt Wood, and on a clear day they are fantastic.

The path descends straight down to the bottom of the field, enters some trees, and meets the Greensand Way. Turn right, following the blue GW bridleway waymarks, but beware mud. Soon, however, the lane widens and becomes surfaced. After some houses turn off right, following a yellow (footpath) GW waymark across fields. Keep close to the woods on your left, and take the lane ahead past a barn and fields of grazing horses. Soon there is a footpath sign pointing half right, up a slope along a field edge. Go past hen coops and a tennis court - and then carry straight on, NOT right, up an inviting lane into woods (this leads to the Chapel of St Mary, an impressive if curious converted hilltop barn that is nevertheless well worth a visit if you have the time). However, the track that you want curves around the slope ahead, above a pond on your left and a pheasant enclosure to the right (these amusing but silly birds are likely to be everywhere).

Go through a field, and where the fence on your right ends there is a GW sign pointing to a half-hidden path among the woods ahead. The clear path is quiet and shaded, and finally it emerges via some bracken on a surfaced lane near Scotsland Farm. Turn right, then left (follow the signs), and up a sunken bridleway which soon swings right. At the very top of the track turn right (the Greensand Way leaves to the left) and follow the path all the way down through brambles and field edges to the road in the bottom of the valley.

CAUTION! The road may not be among the busiest, but the bends either way are tight, so be alert and listen for traffic.

Then go up a rough, steepening lane opposite, which finally levels out by a stand of mature pines. Now follow the surfaced drive ahead to the far end, and there turn right on to a wider lane. Where it meets the B-road once more turn right, and carefully follow the edge for 200m/yds until a public footpath leads off the entrance of the drive of Eden House, opposite. Cross with care. This path then leads directly back to the car park.

WALK 4:
PUTTENHAM COMMON

A straightforward walk over the popular heaths of
Puttenham Common, visiting the village of
Puttenham, where refreshments may be taken, and
returning via the attractive ponds of the Hampton
Park estate. This is very different walking compared
to some of the other chalk-based routes featured.
Here the tracks are dry and sandy, with bracken
and heather predominating, and typical heathland
wildlife includes nightjars, ants and lizards.

Start: Puttenham Common Middle Car Park (east of The Tarn).
GR.913458.
Maps: OS Landranger 186/Pathfinder 1225.
Total distance: 6½km (4 miles).
Height gain: 135m (445 feet).
Difficulty: Easy.

THE WALK:

Leave the car park, where there is a picnic site and information board, by a broad, sandy track north-eastwards in the direction of Puttenham village. Stay on the main path (indicated for the moment by posts with green and purple markings) as it veers half-right then straight ahead at a crossroad of tracks. Keep the open heathland to your right, and after descending to a shaded hollow follow the main sandy track as it climbs gently uphill for a short distance.

Where you meet a major track with telephone wires overhead continue straight on, along a narrow and rather overgrown path among bracken. This is still the same public bridleway that you have been following, and it eventually emerges by a lovely, secluded cottage, with a well-tended and colourful garden.

Take the public footpath

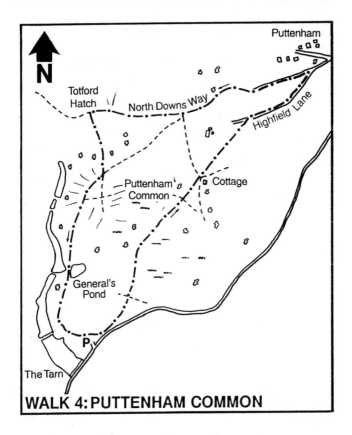

WALK 4: PUTTENHAM COMMON

north-eastwards, indicated by a finger post (NOT the bridleway straight ahead). Go through a gate into a small patch of trees managed by the Woodland Trust.

A sign explains that the gate is dedicated to the memory of Ludovic, Dorothea and Hans-Bernd Jacoby, who died in Auschwitz in 1943.

The path soon emerges by a cottage, and ahead are two successive stiles that lead via fields directly to Highfield Lane and down into Puttenham. To the south-east, across cereal fields, there are great views of the greensand hills beyond

19

Godalming. The lane soon meets another, and you can either turn right into Puttenham (only a minute away) for refreshments, or else turn left and gradually climb up the sunken lane to Little Common. Acorn signs indicate that this is the North Downs Way, a clear and easy track that you should follow for exactly one mile.

To the right are splendid views of the Hog's Back, and its sunny southern slopes that support fruit growing. Beyond Little Common rejoin the main heath, and take the right fork at the official noticeboard. At Totford Hatch, at the bottom of the slope, turn left on to a broad track past a Hampton Estate sign. Follow the track to the right, past a massive, petrified tree, and uphill through bracken. Turn right at a crossroads of tracks to the brow of the hill. The views are splendid, and this may be why a fort was built here in ancient times (there are vague traces of earthworks). The track across the hilltop eastwards allows further views.

Follow the distinctive pathway of red, sandy soil gradually downhill, over another path and then fork right (look out for the posts with purple and green marks on). The mixed woods offer some shade, and in a clearing on the left there are several giant Scots pines. A little further on is General's Pond, on the left, where alder scrub and thicker vegetation can be found. Dragonflies and damselflies buzz over the shallow water and mud.

Finally, the track descends to the shore of The Tarn, where anglers and picnickers vie for space by the attractive, wooded shore. The car park is a couple of minutes away on the track that you have been following, to your left.

ALONG THE WAY:

Heathland: Heather, or ling, is common to any heathland environment, and the large amount of nectar in the purple flowers attracts many bees. Gorse is also widespread, with bright yellow flowers and thorny twigs.

Look out for stonechats and the well-camouflaged nightjar, and if you are very lucky you may even see the rare Dartford warbler.

Yet this distinctive heathland environment is in fact artificial, created abut 6,000 years ago in the late Stone Age when the forest was cleared for farming. Before long the thin, sandy soils became exhausted, and the unique heathland habitat evolved.

WALK 5:
MICKLEHAM DOWNS

This varied walk takes you through mixed woods
and scrub and then over unspoilt chalk downland.
There is an abundance of wildlife, especially moths
and butterflies, including the rare silver-spotted
skipper. Surrey Wildlife Trust's well-managed Nower
Wood can be visited, and some of the route is along
the old Roman road of Stane Street.

Start: Mickleham village. GR.171535.
Bus Route 465 (Kingston-Horsham).
Maps: OS Landranger 187/Pathfinder 1206.
Total distance: 6½km (4 miles).
Height gain: 135m (440 feet).
Difficulty: Easy; one fairly steep descent
(but with bad weather alternative).

THE WALK:

From Mickleham post office, opposite the church, walk north along the pavement and after a few moments turn right into Dell Close. At the end of this cul-de-sac go through a gate, past a sign for Eastfield Cottage, and forwards on to a public footpath among trees. This wide, shaded track high above the Mole valley meets a deserted metalled road. Don't turn right (private) but continue straight ahead along the road for 50m/yds before taking the fork right to Lower Lodge. When this attractive cottage comes into sight there is a small lawn, and to the right you will see a steep flight of 20 wooden steps that disappear into the bushes. At the top of the steps the path levels out, and bushes of violet buddleia and clusters of blackberries line the path. Although there is some yew and silver birch, the messy scrubland once supported a large, mixed wood - until the gale of 1987.

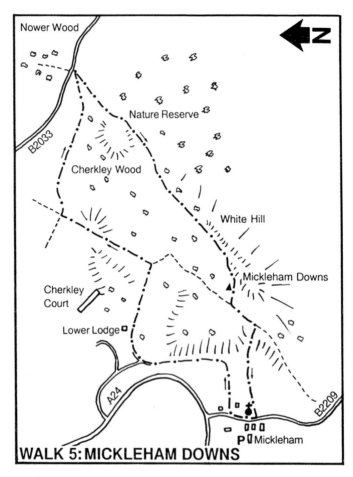

Nower Wood

Nature Reserve

B2033

Cherkley Wood

White Hill

Mickleham Downs

Cherkley
Court

Lower Lodge

A24

B2209

P Mickleham

WALK 5: MICKLEHAM DOWNS

In less than half a mile turn left on to a well-used track. This is Stane Street, a road built by the Romans to connect London to Chichester. Follow its typically straight direction for some time, resisting the urge to take one of several exits into private meadowland to the right. After passing Cherkley Court there is a junction of tracks where you should follow blue bridleway signs to the right, past a golf course and into woodland. At the small car park on the B2033 turn sharply right and back down another signposted bridleway. However, on the far side of the road is Nower Wood, a nature reserve managed by Surrey Wildlife Trust, and this is well worth a visit, since the site includes an exhibition room, nature trails and toilets.

From the bridleway to White Hill there are glimpses of the lovely deciduous woods of Lodge Hill and Box Hill across the valley; then the track emerges on to a strip of open downland bordered by trees and bushes. Horse-riders have to keep behind the white poles, but you can wander unhindered along the open, grassy ridge. At the far end of the hill there is an OS trig point next to some trees. Do not take the path by the side of the trig point, but instead carry on along the grassy path in front of you, which descends into tree cover and to a metal fence. Turn left on to a wide track (Stane Street, once more) and continue downhill.

After passing the National Trust's "Mickleham Downs" sign take a narrow footpath among bushes to the right (indicated by a yellow arrow). Although the path is easy to follow the descent is fairly steep and the vegetation is quite thick at first.

If the chalky ground is wet it may be hazardous, in which case continue down the former track to the valley bottom, turn right, and return to Mickleham along the road - about half a mile. Otherwise, make your way carefully down the path, past a massive, fallen beech tree, and as fields open up on the left the first and only stile on the route leads into a lane that emerges by Mickleham churchyard.

ALONG THE WAY:

Mickleham: A small and quiet community first recorded in the Domesday Book. The odd-shaped, flint exterior of St Michael's Church is worth examining, and opposite is a post office with local tourist information. Nearby, The Running Horses pub serves hot and cold food. Its sign depicts Blair Athol, the 1864 Derby winner that was stabled in the area.

Nower Wood: The reserve consists of 81 acres of broad-leaved woods, where over 70 species of birds have been spotted. The field centre has details on all the other wildlife in the wood, including snakes and deer. There are open days (with guided nature walks) on every third Sunday between April and October, and a visit is highly recommended.

WALK 6:
BANSTEAD WOODS

This is a short and very easy wander through rich, unspoilt woodland, across open farmland, and back via a chalk valley. A whole range of trees and shrubs are on view in Banstead Woods, and in spring the ground is awash with bluebells. There is a seasonal snack bar and public conveniences at the car park.

Start: Car park, Holly Lane, next to Banstead Woods. GR.273583.
Bus routes 166, 498 (Epsom-Croydon) or Chipstead Station.
Maps: OS Landranger 187/Pathfinder 1207.
Total distance: 7km (4½ miles).
Height gain: 90m (295 feet).
Difficulty: Easy.

THE WALK:

Head through the gate and up the wide, gravel track into fine deciduous woodland. Oak, beech and sweet chestnut are just three of the many types to be found, and there are plenty of glades and clearings which give a sense of space and light.

On the left are banks of rhododendron, and on the right you may spot a massive crabapple tree (but its hard and sour fruit is not suitable for eating).

The wide track does not leave the trees (although there is a parallel public footpath out on the grassy hillside to the left), but after nearly a mile the track veers to the right, past a slimy green pond. Ahead, at a T-junction, turn left on to a grassy track and emerge at Perrotts Farm.

Follow the public bridleway sign past the buildings and along an unmade track towards Canons Farm. There are pleasant views across the open fields to Chipstead Valley (south). Approaching Canons

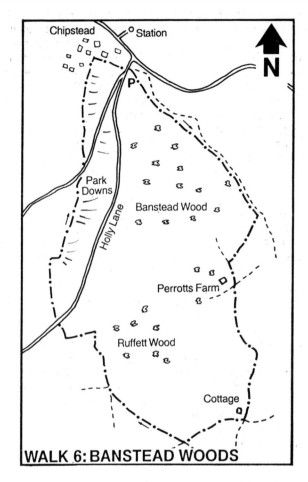

WALK 6: BANSTEAD WOODS

Farm turn right by a cottage on to a footpath and along the left edge of a field. Soon there is a diagonal path half-right across the field, but if the ground is wet or the crops are thick it may be easier to take the former path all the way around the edge to the far right corner.

Once over a couple of stiles and past some pines you come to Ruffett Wood, but since this is private you must follow the footpath along the field edge to the left of it. The last time I walked here this meadow was wild and full of bright red poppies. At the far end the path turns left and across to Holly Lane (first go over another track and through some trees).

The path resumes over the sometimes busy road, and then follow the track above a rising field and on to Park Downs. There are lovely views across this dry chalk valley to Banstead Woods opposite. Enter trees and cross a stile, then carry straight on over other tracks and to the Banstead road. The piece of fenced-off land to your right was where sheep were introduced in order to counter the damaging effect of scrub and course grasses on the rare chalk grassland.

Cross the road carefully, then take the upper of two tracks along the wooded valley top all the way to the end, and at a wooden fence turn right and down to the car park. (Beware! - the path emerges from undergrowth rather suddenly on to the road.)

ALONG THE WAY:

Woodland birds: Apart from the rich variety of trees, many types of birds can be seen. Woodpeckers (green and great spotted) can be heard drilling their way into bark for wood-boring insects, while treecreepers and nuthatches run up and down the trunks in search of food. In the branches you may see willow warblers and chiffchaffs, small and active but rather plain-looking songbirds, but as with all the other varieties keep quiet and still, and use both your eyes and ears. A simple identification book, and perhaps a pair of lightweight binoculars, will assist the aspiring ornithologist.

Ants: As you wander Surrey's rich and varied woodland keep an eye on where you tread. There are about 36 species of ants in Britain, and especially if there are pine trees about, you may see trails of large, brown ants marching across the forest floor, collecting material for their huge nests of twigs and pine needles. But beware - they sting and spray acid when provoked.

WALK 7:
OUTWOOD

Outwood Windmill is the focus of this straightforward and mostly level ramble through woods and over open fields south of Bletchingley. Outwood Windmill is the oldest working windmill in England, and both the mill and its interesting museum are open to the public on Sunday afternoons.

Start: National Trust's Outwood Common car park, near Outwood Windmill. GR.326456.
Maps: OS Landranger 187/Pathfinder 1227.
Total distance: 7km (4½ miles).
Height gain 50m (160 feet).
Difficulty: Easy and flat, but possibly muddy in the woods.

THE WALK:

From the car park off the green in front of the windmill follow the wide track to the cricket green, then just before the pavilion follow a faint path into the trees. Almost immediately turn right, keeping the brook on your left. The path is now clearer, but if it is wet the ground may be muddy. Continue through the woods to first one, then another small footbridge, with steps built into the banks either side, and go forwards up the path. A house soon becomes visible through trees to the left. (To the right, another path leads deep into the woods, and it is possible for the adventurous to follow this westwards, past the church - but there are many other criss-crossing tracks that can confuse).

Emerge on to the road, turn right, and walk the wide, grassy verge a short distance to the handsome Church of St John the Baptist. Just beyond is a signposted bridleway to the right that leads back into the mixed woods of Outwood Common once more. Look out for a massive old oak tree on the right. Its trunk is almost 8 feet wide. How old do you think it is?

The wide track soon comes out by fields, with welcome views towards a low sandstone ridge, and the North Downs beyond. The bridleway itself continues to Burstow Park Farm (and, after that, to the National Trust's Bransland Wood, where there is a small car park if you want to be collected). But you should now go over a stile and follow the yellow public footpath arrow to the right, around and down the edge of a field. From these wide, open fields you may see light aircraft coming in to land at the nearby Redhill Aerodrome, or rather larger planes bound for Gatwick to the south. After more stiles and a footbridge, the path cuts

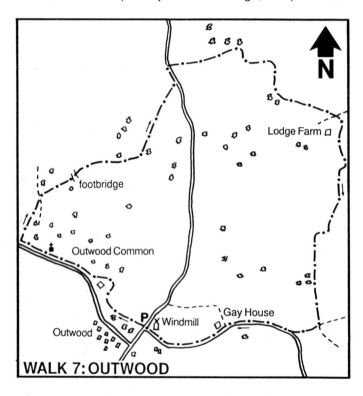

WALK 7: OUTWOOD

diagonally over three successive fields and meets a road.

Opposite is Outwood Swan Sanctuary (where injured swans are taken), and the birds may be glimpsed through the hedge. Turn left on to the road and then right on to a wide farm track. This then follows the left-hand edge of fields past a small oak wood, and soon assumes a very dry and firm gravel surface. Follow its obvious course all the way to Lodge Farm, where it then enters a field to bypass the farm buildings (all waymarked). This field often contains a large flock of geese, wings clipped, and being fattened for Christmas. Follow the blue arrows back into the farm lane, bordered by hedges of blackberry, hawthorn and deadly night-shade. Continue south along this obvious track alongside more fields, and when it finally meets a small copse turn right and after a few moments come out on Gay House Lane.

Turn right and follow the road for half a mile back to Outwood Windmill. This is not usually a busy road, but there is no verge so be careful. If you want to avoid some of the tarmac there is a waymarked footpath across fields to the right, just before Gay House, that emerges at The Bell public house (north of the windmill).

ALONG THE WAY:

Outwood Windmill: Built in 1665, Outwood Windmill is the oldest working mill in the country, and it is said that the year after the mill was built the residents of Outwood could see the glow of the Great Fire of London from the top, approximately 27 miles away. Outwood is a post mill, which means that the entire mill is balanced on one fixed, central post (known as the king post). This allows the miller to turn the whole mill to face whichever direction the wind is blowing from, so that the pair of 59-foot sails can turn and the wheat is ground into flour. The windmill, with an accompanying rural museum and small collection of farm animals, is open to the public every Sunday from Easter to the end of October, 2.00pm - 6.00pm (daily and evening tours can be arranged by appointment).

WALK 8:
EPSOM DOWNS

Although located a few miles away from the others, this gentle walk covers fine Surrey downland, plus undulating fields and copses, and offers many good views. It begins and ends at the famous race-course, which encircles the downs, and since it is likely that you will meet horses out being trained make sure that you are watchful when crossing the marked gallops. (This walk is probably not a good idea on race days, when access may be restricted.)

Start: Any one of the car parks at top of race course (off B290). GR.224585.
Bus Routes 406,727 (Kingston, Epsom and Redhill services) or Tattenham Corner Station.
Maps: OS Landranger 187/Pathfinder 1207.
Total distance: 7km (4½ miles).
Height gain: 125m (410 feet).
Difficulty: Easy.

THE WALK:

Cross the race track south-wards by the small road, then follow the wide bridle-way that sweeps across the open downs ahead. To the right the race track dips down to the huge white grandstand in the distance, an impressive spectacle. Where the bridle-way meets the race track at the far side model aircraft enthusiasts are often to be found. Cross the track once more and turn left. Almost immediately turn right, following a footpath sign into woodland. After a short while this path emerges on to Walton Downs, and on to the edge of some wide, grassy gallops that slope away before you. Turn left and walk a short distance to the beginning of some white railings.

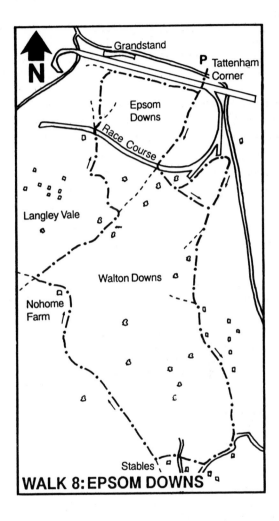

WALK 8: EPSOM DOWNS

The gallops are used for the training of racehorses, and if they are thundering up and down then keep a safe and respectful distance, and reach the track at the bottom of the slope by walking around by the rails and the hedge at the top of the field. (Notices state that the horses are usually exercised between 6.00am and mid-day.) If there are no horses about then go across the grass by the faint path directly before you, and turn right on to the wide track at the bottom. Soon woodland appears, and here turn off left on a public bridleway into the undergrowth (ignore the sign pointing walkers to the right of the horse-only tracks.)

After some pleasant woodland, the houses of Tadworth appear on the left and arable fields on the right. Continue along the clear track in between, and eventually arrive at an unsurfaced lane. Turn right, and follow this for a short distance, admiring the views back to Walton Downs, then turn right once more on to a signposted footpath by stables. Continue through a field, over a lane, until after another field and yet more stables you can turn right on to a firm bridleway.

For nearly a mile this lovely, direct track canters along the crest of the hill, between fields of grazing horses, and then crops, and with fine views of rolling, mixed woodland towards Ashtead and Headley. Eventually it drops down via the curiously-named Nohome Farm, and curves left. Continue for a couple of minutes, then turn half right through wooden rails, and up into woodland. Where the path emerges by gallops join a wide bridleway across the gallops before you and continue up the hill above them. After the trees have begun to close in look for a white bar gate on the left, and take a waymarked footpath across a field to more woods. Turn right on to another path, then continue straight ahead, via a children's playground and small clearing.

When you finally arrive at a wide, popular track turn left, and continue down this past the ends of three residential roads. When the track rises it meets more gallops. Cross and follow a faint path ahead and up over the coarse grass. The path skirts bushes on the left, then all of a sudden Epsom Downs is once more revealed.

You are on a public footpath, and this now legitimately crosses the racetrack and heads over the downs towards the massive grandstand. Near the finishing post, and the odd metal gantry rising out of the long grass (which is used to hoist up the numbers of the winning horses and the betting odds), turn right and follow the trackside drive back up to the car park.

Epsom Downs

The south-facing scarp of the North Downs may be more dramatic, but where the chalk slopes gently northwards towards London there is also much of interest, in particular the high ground around Banstead and Epsom used for grazing animals. Sheep were once reared here, and the wool from Banstead Downs was highly regarded.

From the 1600s, however, the training and racing of horses became a more common activity, and in 1683 Charles II came to watch the racing. Although horses had been raced on the firm turf above the former spa town of Epsom for some years, it was not until the 12th Earl of Derby established two famous races that Epsom Downs became well-known. The Oaks was first run in 1779, and was named after his house near Carshalton (destroyed in an air raid in 1944). The Derby, established a year later, is now the more famous of the two. The race itself is over in just 1½ minutes, but it is all the razzmatazz surrounding the event that people enjoy; and such has been its popularity over the years that in 1921 traffic congestion was so bad around Epsom that an airship and RAF squadron had to be called in to control the traffic! Derby Day regularly attracts tens of thousands of spectators every year, and has become a world-famous event, with open-top buses, picnics, fun-fairs, vendors, gypsy fortune-tellers, marquees, and much more.

WALK 9:
SHERE

The route is essentially up and then back down - from the attractive village of Shere (or Gomshall if you are taking the train) up on to and then along the wooded downs, then a return to the valley floor and a gentle amble through farmland and via lanes. On Hackhurst Downs you may see orchids and butterflies, while great tits and warblers sing in the woods. Below flows the Tilling Bourne, quietly through Shere, noisily at Gomshall Mill, as well as feeding the nearby watercress beds at Abinger Hammer.

Start: Shere village. GR.078473.
Bus Routes 21, 22, 25, 433,448, 525, 588 (Guildford, Dorking and Cranleigh services) or Gomshall Station.
Maps: OS Landranger 187/Pathfinder 1226.
Total distance: 7½km (4¾ miles).
Height gain: 180m (590 feet).
Difficulty: Most of the surfaces are firm and level, but there is one, very long uphill track on to the downs that some younger walkers may find tiring.

THE WALK:

Starting from the centre of Shere, walk north up Middle Street until the T-junction, then turn left and immediately right on to the driveway to Shere Recreational Ground. Do not enter the playing fields but instead take the byway ahead/ left into woods. This sunken, rutted track passes beneath the A25 and climbs steadily up the hillside. Soon veer right at a fork, and continue uphill by the National Trust's Netley Park. The chalk track drains easily, and where the vegetation parts there are superb

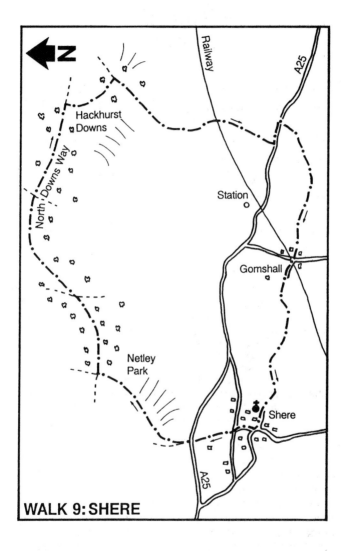

WALK 9: SHERE

views over Shere to Hurt Wood.

Finally, the track levels out by some beautiful beech trees, and at a crossroads of paths turn right on to a wide bridleway. This is the North Downs Way (watch out for the small black and white acorn sign, which denotes a National Trail). Follow the wide and direct, semi-surfaced track for over a mile, to Hackhurst Downs. (If you want to shorten the walk turn right at Gravehill Gate and take Colekitchen Lane down into Gomshall.) Where the mixed woods part there are good views, and the occasional picnic table.

Approaching Hackhurst Downs follow the acorn sign down a short path to the right, past Surrey County Council's handy bench, and downhill over open ground. The path swings left (ignore a stile and gate off right) and before long emerges on a wide lane. Wave goodbye to the North Downs Way and head down the straight, firm byway known as Beggar's Lane.

There are handsome views over the Tilling Bourne valley, as fields open up either side. At the bottom the lane crosses under the railway and eventually comes out on the A25. Cross this busy road with EXTREME CARE, then turn left and follow the pavement for a few hundred yards until turning right by a public bridleway signpost on to an unsurfaced lane.

At the end of this take the right of two bridleways (under a lovely archway of holly) which ends by a row of houses. Turn right and follow the lane for a few minutes, then where it curves sharply right take a narrow path on the left by a fenced field. At the end of this join a surfaced road and go under the railway bridge, then left at a junction (or turn right here if you wish to visit/return to Gomshall). At the next junction carry on straight ahead (Gravelpits Lane), then to the right of the farmhouse along an unsurfaced lane. Soon you are walking along field edges, with excellent views across to Netley Park. To reach Shere, now visible below, take the obvious path down to the handsome Norman church.

ALONG THE WAY:

Shere: One of Surrey's most picturesque, and popular, villages. There is plenty to interest everyone: resident white ducks paddle up and down the Tilling Bourne, which flows amid old timber-framed houses, and below the well-preserved St James's Church (it dates from around 1190 AD). The White Horse Inn is itself over 400 years old, or else refreshment may be had at one of the rather newer tearooms.

Gomshall Mill: There has been a mill on this site since the time of the Domesday Book, although the present building dates from mid-17th century. It now houses a café and gift shops, but the huge iron mill wheels have been fully restored, and are a fascinating sight as the waters of the Tilling Bourne tumble over.

The Great Storm of 1987

The 100 mph winds that battered the South of England one October night uprooted or damaged over 15 million trees, with Surrey being one of the worst affected counties. On a number of walks you will see untidy areas of shrub, bushes and scattered, isolated trees, all that remains of once mature and extensive woodland.

But, as is often the case with Nature, good did come out of the destruction. The storm removed many old or diseased trees, allowing younger, more vigorous specimens to grow, and made room for new saplings to spring up. The masses of rotting wood on the ground and the space and light created by the fallen trees encouraged the growth of wild flowers. Insects, too, prospered, especially the host of beetles that live on and in decaying wood. This in turn provided more food for birds, bats, and other creatures, as well as new opportunities for nest sites.

The skyline of Reigate Hill and Mickleham Downs may have been dramatically altered overnight, but amid the chaos came new life and fresh beginnings.

WALK 10:
REIGATE AND COLLEY HILLS

A straightforward circuit of the North Downs
above Reigate, first down to its wooded foot and
along the ancient Pilgrims' Way, then back on to
the brow. There are superlative views across the
county from the open top of Colley Hill, via the
North Downs Way.

Start: Car park, top of Reigate Hill. GR.263523.
Bus Routes 406, 420, 422, 520, 727. (Kingston, Banstead and
Sutton services).
Maps: OS Landranger 187/Pathfinder 1207.
Total distance: 9½km (6 miles).
Height gain: 210m (690 feet).
Difficulty: There is a potentially slippery descent down a steep, narrow
path; otherwise the tracks should be clear and fairly firm.

THE WALK:

Leave the car park, snack bar and toilets via a high footbridge across the A217 for a wide track to Reigate Hill. Where it meets a metalled lane and cottages turn left, down a public bridleway. Ignore a path to the right and stay with the narrowing and steepening sunken track as it heads down through woodland. (This section may be slippery after bad weather.) At the bottom it emerges on the main road, and although you follow the pavement for only a few paces before turning right at another signposted bridle-way ("No Through Road") be extremely careful of speeding traffic.

Almost immediately the lane forks. Take the rough track past houses to the left, which is soon enclosed by walls. Where it meets a junction of lanes go straight over and along a drive of posh, hedged-off houses, then ahead through a gate bearing a National Trust sign. This announces that the track is in fact the Pilgrims' Way, a medieval pilgrims travelling from Winchester to Canterbury Cathedral.

Follow the track around the foot of the wooded downs (it veers right, then soon left). Stay with the main path, and at a wooded combe go up steps and straight on until you are walking under a dense canopy of yew trees below Colley Hill. At a junction of tracks the North Downs Way joins from the right. Continue straight on, and gaps in the trees allow superb views towards Box Hill, with its white, gaping chalk quarries particularly noticeable.

Stay with the National Trail acorn symbols westwards (ignore a bridleway left) until a short but steep descent to a wide, rough lane. Turn right and follow this up the hill (the North Downs Way leaves at this point). Nearing the top take a bridleway on the right, and follow this level track through woodland. After it passes a field turn left on to a fenced track

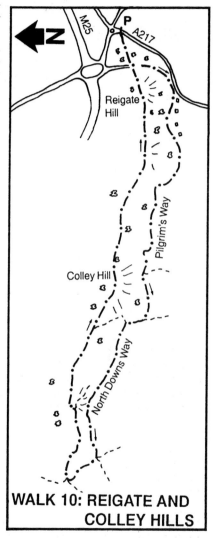

WALK 10: REIGATE AND COLLEY HILLS

(resist the temptation to carry straight on). Quickly right once more, then straight on along the partly wooded top of the downs.

Maintain an easterly direction, between hedged-off gardens and stables, and with the muffled roar of the M25 in the background. When you emerge at the end of a surfaced drive by Juniper Cottage ignore the path with the acorn sign ahead/right (this is the North Downs way coming up/going down the hill!). Instead, turn left then right, following NDW finger posts for a firm and level track to the National Trust sign at the top of Colley Hill. Here, turn right and out on to the lovely, open downs. There are tremendous views from this lofty viewpoint: Reigate, Gatwick Airport, Leith Hill, and even to the South Downs on a clear day. Wander over the turf eastwards heading for a small, temple-like construction known as The Horseshoe in the far corner, and follow the North Downs Way back to Reigate Hill and the car park.

ALONG THE WAY:

The North Downs Way: The country's eighth National Trail was officially opened in September 1978, and runs for 246km (153 miles) from Farnham in Surrey to Dover in Kent, with an additional loop via Canterbury. Although the first few miles of the North Downs Way are over sandy heathland, most of the route sticks to the distinctive chalk ridge of the North Downs - from which its sister route, the South Downs Way, is often visible - and the attractive chalk grassland usually supports a wide range of wild flowers and butterflies. For a walking route so close to London it is surprisingly rural, but at the same time the excellent transport links makes this a route that can easily be walked over single days or weekends.

Ordnance Survey maps for Surrey frequently show the name 'Pilgrims' Way' along the edge of the North Downs, but in reality there is no continuous, waymarked walking trail on the ground. However, the ancient route of travellers between the two cathedral cities can still be followed for around 80 of its 120 miles, albeit along modern roads and lanes, as well as some tracks and paths.

See: *National Trail Guide: North Downs Way* by Neil Curtis (Aurum Press) and *Guide to the Pilgrims' Way and North Downs Way* by C J Wright (Constable Books).

WALK 11:
FRENSHAM

Surrey's unspoilt heathland is unique and fascinating, and this walk explores two large lakes that are rich in wildlife, with opportunities for picnics by the water's edge. There are good views from modest elevation, and the tracks are wide and sandy.

Start: Car park, Frensham Common. GR.845405.
Bus Routes 19, 519 (Aldershot-Haslemere).
Maps: OS Landranger 186/Pathfinder 1225 & 1245.
Total distance: 8km (5 miles).
Height gain: 75m (250 feet).
Difficulty: No sharp gradients, but deep, sandy tracks may make the going slow.

THE WALK:

Next to the car park are toilets and a snack bar, plus an information room, staffed for most of the year by a warden. Vehicular access is no longer from the A287 but to the north of the Great Pond, off the minor road to the Frensham Ponds Hotel.

Head back down the short drive of the car park and turn right on to bridleway 45 (look for their numbers on small blue-topped posts). Soon fork right on to bridleway 43, then drop down and cross the A287 with care. Follow the track opposite to the crest of a low hill. Use a firmer path on the right if the deep, sandy furrows of the bridleway make progress difficult.

The views from the top are extensive for such a modest height. South-west lie Frensham Great Pond and the River Wey; immediately to the north-east is the Little Pond; and turning south-east you can see the wooded bumps known as the Devil's Jumps, with the forested Beacon Hill and Hindhead beyond.

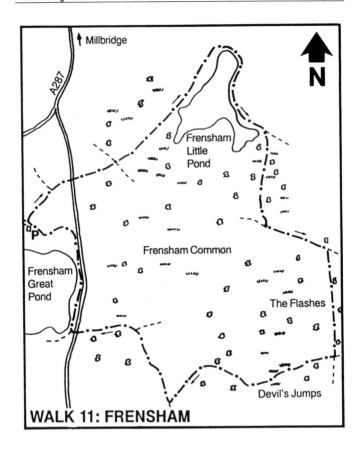

↑ Millbridge

Frensham
Little
Pond

Frensham Common

Frensham
Great
Pond

The Flashes

Devil's Jumps

WALK 11: FRENSHAM

From the many paths on offer, take the one that heads directly for Frensham Little Pond, a small but attractive lake that is surrounded by patchy woodland and reedbeds. At the bottom of the slope cross a bridleway, and keeping the fence on your right, follow the clear path around the Pond's western shore. At the head of the water is a lovely stand of pines, with a large and inviting sandy beach that allows access to the waterside. No boating is permitted, since much of the Little Pond is devoted to wildlife, but fishing is popular with both humans (the Farnham Angling Society) and birds (look out for herons).

At the National Trust cottages and car park turn right along the lane for a few yards, then back to the water's edge via a path. Follow this all the way along the eastern shore, among buzzing dragonflies, until the path veers left, by a plantation of young Christmas trees. At a National Trust sign turn sharp right. The reedy, southern end of the pond is visible through bushes. At a junction of paths keep left - do NOT cross the footbridge - and follow this through woodland for some time.

Where the path emerges on to a surfaced but deserted forest road turn left (ignore the bridleway) and take this as far as Woodmans Cottage. Now turn right on to bridleway 40 through an area known as The Flashes, with shallow ponds and scrubby heathland. Ahead are the Devil's Jumps. These are three very small wooded hills (big conical lumps, really), which the Devil is said to have once jumped along. There is a public footpath to the summit of the eastern one (on the left as you look at them), should you want to admire the views.

At a junction of tracks bear right and take bridleway P5

along the foot of the hills. Soon extensive views over open heathland are revealed on your right. This wide and obvious track continues for almost a mile until it meets a surfaced lane. Turn right, and when the lane peters out continue along the rising dirt track straight ahead. A National Trust sign announces that you are re-entering Frensham Common, and here take a bridleway left, which runs down to the road.

Take care crossing the A287 once more. It can be busy, so hold small hands. Once on the bridleway, opposite, turn off right, through some wooden barriers, and back via a scenic track along the shore of the Great Pond to the car park.

ALONG THE WAY:
The Frensham Ponds: The two ponds are in fact artificial, created in the 12th century to provide fish for the Bishop of Winchester (he lived in nearby Farnham Castle), and by the 17th century Frensham carp were apparently much sought after at London fish markets.

In 1913 the world's first sea plane was tested on the Great Pond; then during the Second World War the lakes were drained to prevent them becoming landmarks for German bombers heading for Aldershot.

Caring for the heath: Frensham Common is a Site of Special Scientific Interest, and is one of only two places in the country with native populations of all six British reptiles, including the rare sand lizard. But much work is needed to maintain this delicate habitat. As you cross the heath you may see small strips where the ground has been totally cleared. This encourages specialised plants and rare insects, such as the tiger beetle, to develop. Elsewhere, cattle have been introduced in order to protect the heath by grazing on young trees and crushing bracken shoots that might otherwise ruin the habitat of the indigenous heathland wildlife.

Dragonflies: There are 25 species of dragonfly in Britain. They have two pairs of large wings, and are usually found near water where they prey on mosquitoes and other insects (they are harmless to humans!). Look out for the brightly-coloured Broad Bodied Chaser, and the distinctive blue Emperor dragonfly.

Food and drink for walking
Whether or not you enjoy picnics, any walk in the countryside is enhanced by having something to munch and a refreshing drink. But most importantly it provides the energy every walker needs. But what exactly should you take?
In summer a cool drink, and plenty of it, is vital. Water and squash is better than fizzy drinks, and snacks such as apples, raisins and flapjack or cereal bars are more nourishing than crisps and peanuts. Sandwiches and rolls (filled with cheese, marmite, fishpaste, or jam etc) are better than pies and pasties which are high in fat and take a long time to digest. In winter the main requirement is to keep warm, so a flask of hot tea, coffee or, even better, hot soup, is perfect.

WALK 12:
ST MARTHA'S HILL

A varied walk around St Martha's Hill, east of
Guildford. There is a wooded descent to former
gunpowder mills by the attractive Tilling Bourne
river (the ruins of some of the workings can still be
seen), then fieldside paths connect with the North
Downs Way as it strides back across the crest of
the downs via St Martha's Church.

Start: Car park, Guildford Lane (north west of Albury). GR.036485.
Maps: OS Landranger 186/Pathfinder 1226.
Total distance: 9½km (6 miles).
Height gain: 210m (690 feet).
Difficulty: Moderate, with some short, steep sections. Most of the paths
are firm. Several chances to shorten the route.

THE WALK:

Go a short distance up the bridleway from the car park and turn south, down a clear footpath amongst bracken towards the valley bottom. The sunken path steepens, and may be slippery after rain. As you pass under a roof of beech trees a gurgling stream appears below. The path swings left and levels out, and descends through Colyers Hanger to Waterloo Pond.

Turn left and follow a path clockwise around the quiet pond - but if you want to cut down on distance turn right instead and omit the diversion. Now walk along the surfaced lane to Albury Mill, by Potsford Pond, which usually has some distinctive Muscovy ducks. Take the signposted public footpath alongside a fence ahead, with wide, open fields gradually appearing. Go over a stile and through a small field to a rough lane. Turn right then immediately left, and follow a firm track by the waters of the Tilling Bourne. The old buildings on the right

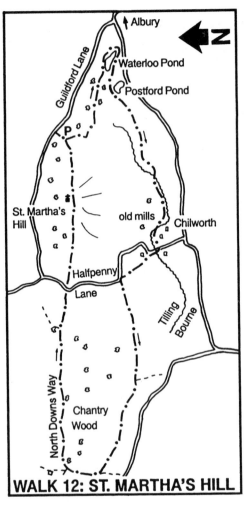

WALK 12: ST. MARTHA'S HILL

Gunpowder Mills (there is an information board with sketches nearby).

Keep to the main path parallel to the stream, ignoring other tracks off, and emerge by West Lodge, the entrance to the former factory. Turn right on to the road, and then where it curves right take the signposted footpath to the left. (If you continue along the road there is soon a bridleway to Chilworth Manor, then a footpath to St Martha's Hill, which effectively shortens the distance of the overall walk by half). When the path comes out at a road corner turn left into an arable field, and follow a footpath along its left edge. There are good views of the eastern end of the Hog's Back and the Wey valley.

include a charcoal mill, "incorporating" mills and a boiler house - all that remains of the once important Chilworth

Keep to the field edge past Manor Farm, then with the outskirts of Guildford approaching the track crosses a field in the direction of Guildford Cathedral (not the green spire of Shalford Church). Turn right into a residential road, then ahead up a track past Chantry Wood. At Chantry Cottage turn right into a wide, unsurfaced lane - the North Downs Way (as well as the far more ancient Pilgrims' Way) - and follow this for almost a mile, with lovely woodland on the right and fields of grazing horses to the left.

When you enter woods, follow the National Trail acorn waymarks straight on (NOT the bridleway to the left). At Halfpenny Lane turn left then right by Southern Way Cottage, and up a wide track to the Church of St Martha's on the Hill. This small building dates from Norman times, but was rebuilt in 1850, and from its height of 175m (573 feet) there are splendid views of Blackheath Common and the greensand hills of south-west Surrey.

Continue past the church and down the wide, sandy track. A noticeboard explains that the Downs Link, a 48km (30-mile) walking route that follows an abandoned railway line all the way to the South Downs at Steyning begins here. The car park is just a little further on. (For those with any energy left consider a romp across Albury Downs to Newlands Corner, over the other side of the lane.)

ALONG THE WAY:
Chilworth Gunpowder Mills:
From 1625-1920 this was one of the most important gunpowder-producing sites in the country. The alder trees by the river were burnt to make charcoal for the gunpowder, and the river itself was dammed in order to power what at one time were as many as 16 powder mills.

In the First World War several thousand people were employed here (and it was at this time that St Martha's Church on the hilltop above was covered with fir branches to prevent it being used as a landmark by German Zeppelins seeking to bomb the gunpowder mills). Today the tall chimneys have gone; but a few ruined mills are still evident in the woods by the path, and there is also the site of a swingbridge that carried a tramway over the stream on your left.

WALK 13:
DEVIL'S PUNCHBOWL

The Devil's Punchbowl is a well-known Surrey beauty spot, and this walk begins at the head of the large, unspoilt sandstone valley - the Punchbowl - then wanders down the wooded western edge towards the village of Thursley. The return is via lovely mixed woodland and open heath, with more stunning views, and a path that explores the valley bottom prior to a sharp final ascent.

Start: National Trust car park, Hindhead. GR.892358.
Bus Routes 18, 19, 271, 518, 571 (Haslemere, Aldershot and Guildford services).
Maps: OS Landranger 186/Pathfinder 1245.
Total distance: 8km (5 miles).
Height gain: 195m (640 feet).
Difficulty: There is a short climb up the final slope, otherwise the gradients are gentle and the surfaces mostly firm.

THE WALK:

The car park is situated beside the Hillcrest Café and public toilets, and from here the high southern rim of the Punchbowl is only a few strides away. Pause and admire the views, then turn left (north-west) and follow the clear bridleway through woodland past Hindhead.

At a junction of tracks continue ahead (under a vehicle height barrier) and NOT down the path to the right.

The wide forest track sweeps confidently along, until a small path off to the right through the Scots pines leads to the National Trust's Highcomb Copse memorial, with fabulous views across the Punchbowl. The path soon rejoins the bridleway, and when the main track curves sharply to the right, down into the trees, go straight on, past a post bearing a blue bridleway arrow. Now the track descends a narrow, sunken corridor among holly bushes and dark vegetation.

Finally, emerge at the corner of Hyde Lane, and turn right, up a rough lane past Ridgeway Farm. This then dips muddily down to cross a lovely stream by a footbridge in a quiet, hidden dell. Turn off left over a stile and into a rising field. The path sticks to the left-hand fence, before squeezing between fields, with views over Frensham Common to Farnham.

At Hedge

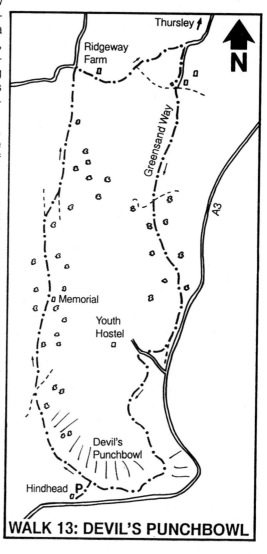

WALK 13: DEVIL'S PUNCHBOWL

Farm the village of Thursley is only a few minutes walk away (either along the quiet road, or a longer footpath route via Smallbrook), and here the Three Horseshoes serves refreshments. Otherwise, from Hedge Farm follow the No Through Road to Little Cowdray Farm, then straight ahead on a wide, unsurfaced byway (denoted by the red waymark). Continue past the National Trust's Devil's Punchbowl sign and over a cattle grid by fencing, since sheep and New Forest ponies are being grazed in this area to cut back invasive plants and encourage the growth of natural heather. Where the beech-lined sunken lane forks, go uphill, half-left, following red byway arrows marked GW (this is part of the Greensand Way long distance footpath).

The track soon emerges from the bracken and silver birch to reveal wonderful views across the Punchbowl, but this time from its eastern rim. Soon there are extensive views the other way, towards Hambledon and the North Downs. The bridleway descends to the edge of the A3, but stay well back from this dangerous racetrack, and instead continue on the same path down the hillside and on to a surfaced lane to the youth hostel in the valley bottom.

Before reaching the hostel there is a post on the left with a yellow arrow, amid holly trees, and this clear and attractive footpath leads you all the way along the open valley floor, finally curving right for a short but sharp pull back up to the head of the Punchbowl. Turn right and return to the initial viewpoint by the car park.

The Devils' Punchbowl: This huge natural amphitheatre was known to the Anglo-Saxons as Wolf's Den, and when the weather is rough and mist swirls about the tree tops there is still a wild feel about the place. Hindhead Common used to be the haunt of smugglers and highwaymen, and for a century or so travellers on the London-Portsmouth road, which climbs the eastern edge of the Punchbowl, sometimes ran a dangerous gauntlet. In the late summer and autumn the Devil's Punchbowl is a beautiful spectacle, with the contrasting colours of pine, oak, ash and birch on one side of the valley, and flowering heather and gorse spread over the open heathland on the other. For the energetic the 272m summit of nearby Gibbet Hill is also worth a visit, with tremendous views towards Sussex and the South Downs.

WALK 14:
PEASLAKE

The clear and sandy woodland tracks offer surprise escarpment views and make this an attractive walk. Winterfold Forest and Hurt Wood comprise mainly birch and pine, much of it natural woodland, and wildlife includes woodpeckers, roe deer and wood ants. Pitch Hill and Holmbury Hill both allow panoramic views southwards over the Weald, and the grassy tops are ideal picnic spots.

Start: Car park, Pond Lane, Peaslake (although the route also passes through four Hurt Wood Control car parks, any one of which can be a convenient start/finish point). GR.086448.
Bus Route 25 (Guildford-Cranleigh).
Maps: OS Landranger 187/Pathfinder 1226.
Total distance: 11½km (7 miles).
Height gain: 335m (1100 feet).
Difficulty: Quite long, with many ups and downs, some of them steep.

THE WALK:

From Hurtwood Inn follow the road, appropriately-named Walking Bottom, past St Mark's Church up the hill. Hurtwood Control Car Park No 1 is on the left. After a few minutes turn off, right, on to a drive then bridleway, signposted Bentley Copse. Go past Peaslake House along a clear track into Hurt Wood. Once through a lovely pine wood pass Bentley Copse scout camp and cross a surfaced road (take extreme care - traffic approaches around semi-blind bends), and off the lane opposite take a clearly indicated bridleway to the left. The sandy track cuts through bracken and patchy trees, with heather skirting the path, and along here you may see the occasional roe deer.

Near Dewdney's Well, hidden in the trees, go through a gate,

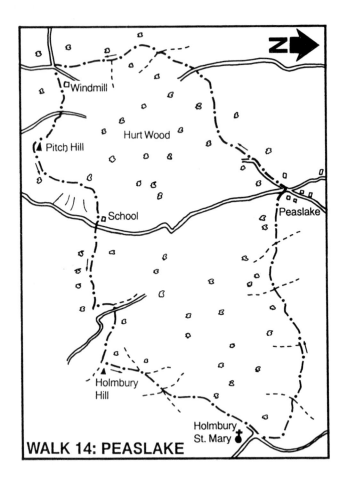

WALK 14: PEASLAKE

and then at a junction of wide forest tracks take the one directly ahead that curves left through Winterfold Forest. The small birds in the conifers may include goldcrests and members of the tit family.

After a gentle climb go through a gate and on to a narrower path under tree cover. When it emerges at Car Park No 4, turn left over the road and up a path bearing a Greensand Way sign. Follow the course of this 106-mile long-distance footpath past Ewhurst Windmill, now a private residence, and down a sunken path (by the fence on the right), which may be slippery in wet weather.

At Car Park No 3, turn right and take the waymarked footpath through gorse bushes to Pitch Hill. At first it is rather steep, past a large sand quarry, but the effort is worth it, since the views from the 257m top are superb. Leave by a clear path north-eastwards towards Hurt Wood. Fork right, and once through the saplings and bracken, drop down to a bridleway and past some hedged-off houses. After a short distance take a public footpath off to the right, and down past the elegant buildings of the Duke of Kent School (for independent boarders).

At the end of the drive there is a narrow path opposite, again marked 'GW' (Greensand Way), which squeezes through fields of horses, cows and sheep for a quarter of a mile, then climbs through scrub to Car Park No 1. Follow the yellow permissive path sign to the right, and this

eventually leads to the breezy summit of Holmbury Hill, a terrific viewing station.

From the trig point take the obvious but unwaymarked track north. It becomes very wide, and where it is crossed by another, fork right. At the 5-way junction of routes on Somerset Hill take the second exit from the left. This shaded, sloping path emerges by the village hall at Holmbury St Mary, where a lane leads to the village green and The Royal Oak public house (which serves food).

From the green there is a narrow path up the hillside between the red telephone box and overgrown cemetery which veers right into woodland. Soon it becomes clearer, and you should keep to this main route eastwards for a mile and a half, to Peaslake. Ignore crisscrossing paths, keep a murky-looking pool on your left, and at a meeting of tracks, under a massive old beech tree, go straight on so that open fields emerge on your right.

To enter Peaslake either follow the tarmac lane down to the left, or else there is a short-cut down a steep and potentially slippery path.

WALK 15:
FARTHING DOWNS AND CHALDON

The downland and dry valleys of a chalk landscape always make for interesting and enjoyable walking, especially when - like here - they provide an escape for so many south London families. There are birds and butterflies in Happy Valley, an ancient church at Chaldon, and views over the Weald from the crest of the North Downs. Much of the route described follows the efficiently-waymarked Downlands Circular Walks (3 or 7 miles long), and there are several points where the overall walk can be shortened.

Start: Car park, north end of Farthing Downs. GR.300584.
Maps: OS Landranger 187/Pathfinder 1207.
Total distance: 13km (8 miles).
Height gain: 160m (530 feet).
Difficulty: Although quite a long walk there are no particularly steep gradients; but some of the bridleways may be muddy.

THE WALK:

Go south along the narrow, grassy top of Farthing Downs as far as the keepers' cottages. There is a display board opposite a car park and toilets (start from this point if you want to shorten the overall walk). The signpost near the board points down a wide track into Devilsden Wood. Follow this into and along the edge of Happy Valley, a lovely, hidden grassy valley among the woods. Already you will have seen the distinctive flower symbol (the greater yellow rattle) and coloured arrows of the Downlands Walk - look out for them if you are uncertain of direction.

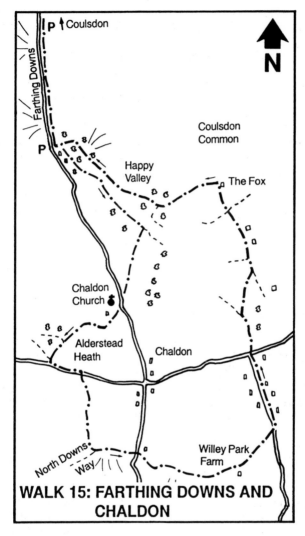

WALK 15: FARTHING DOWNS AND CHALDON

Stay on the western edge of Happy Valley until a path is indicated to the right, to Chaldon Church. A sign asks you to follow the path across the field in single file since it is a "working farm" - but that is rather obvious as you walk between the cereal crops. Cross the lane at the far side and stop to inspect the 1000-year-old Church of St Peter and St Paul, but do take muddy boots off first if you go inside to see the famous wall painting.

Beyond the church go over a stile and follow well-trodden paths through then around several fields to Alderstead Heath. As you enter the trees turn left (the waymarked walk goes straight on) and follow a concrete pathway for a short distance before turning left and, re-entering the field, take a permissive path parallel with the road until you reach a kissing gate. Cross the road with the utmost care - it can be busy - and follow the lane opposite past the handsome Tollsworth Manor Farm until you meet the North Downs Way puffing its way up across fields from Merstham. Turn left and join its hilltop route. There are extensive views from this stretch: the buzzing motorways (M25 and M23) and the Redhill-Reigate sprawl, and in the distance the forested ridges of the Weald.

Cross a minor road and pass some large houses, then at the "three-ways" signpost the Downlands Walk turns left. Should you want a shorter circuit then do the same, returning to Happy Valley via Rook Lane, Doctors Lane and Piles Wood - follow the signs. Otherwise, continue along the North Downs Way until a junction of lanes just past Willey Park Farm. Take the left turning, down to Roffes Lane, admiring the fine views north over London (the Crystal Palace transmitters, Canary Wharf and the City are all visible). Here turn sharply left, into Chaldon Common Road, a wide, quiet residential street. At the end cross the Caterham road with care for a signposted footpath along the right edge of a large field. Before long the trees on the right thin, and a field entrance reveals a footpath that dips down then rises through the pasture in the direction of some new homes. A bridleway runs alongside them, and take this (left) past Caterham barracks to Coulsdon Common. When you reach the common carry straight on to The Fox (hot and cold food, tea and coffee).

Continue beyond the pub, where an obvious tarmac path leads past a Trim Trail (a series of outdoor exercise stations for those with any energy left) and back to the eastern edge of Happy Valley. Descend the path to the valley bottom, and resume the remainder of the Downlands

Walk. The valley's open grass spaces and picnic tables are simply crying out to be enjoyed; and the meadows contain a variety of wildflowers and butterflies - have an identification book handy.

After about a mile the wide, direct track veers to the left and up through scattered woodland to the open turf of Farthing Downs once more. The car park is across the downs to your right.

ALONG THE WAY:
Conserving Farthing Downs:
The fences and cattle grids on top of Farthing Downs are due to the re-introduction of grazing cattle, a move designed to manage the sensitive chalk grassland in a traditional manner. The cattle help to keep at bay coarse grasses and encroaching scrub (that is, bushes and young trees that would soon invade the open grass), which in turn encourages the growth of natural chalk grassland flowers. Look out for the small yellow petals of cowslip and horseshoe vetch, and the white heads of daisies.

The Church of St Peter and St Paul, Chaldon: This handsome medieval building contains the earliest known English wall painting. Dating from around 1200 AD, it was only discovered in 1870 after being hidden for centuries by dirt and other surfaces. The mural was probably the work of an artist monk, possibly from Canterbury, and depicts the struggle between good and evil - a classic theme in religious works of art. It shows two worlds: the lower one is a version of Hell, where the wicked are forever tormented by devilish figures; but above is a happier world of peace and goodness where Christ and the Angels live. The two worlds are joined by the 'ladder of salvation', but to climb it - and leave the Devil for the Angels - is not an easy task. Mere mortals have first to turn their backs on the seven deadly sins, all depicted in the painting: avarice (greed), envy, lust, pride, anger, gluttony and sloth (laziness).

WALK 16:
HAMBLEDON

First a short walk to Hambledon Church and the top of Vann Hill, then down to gentle fields and woodland as this easy and varied walk makes use of firm farm tracks. A short detour to Dunsfold is possible, before the return leg via the ancient Wealden woodland of Hambledon Hurst.

Start: Car park opposite The Merry Harriers, north of Hambledon village (or by church). GR.967392.
Maps: OS Landranger 186/Pathfinder 1245.
Total distance: 12km (7½ miles).
Height gain: 200m (655 feet).
Difficulty: Easy, with few gradients, although some of the woodland paths may be muddy and slippery.

THE WALK:

Leave the car park and camp site by the adjoining public footpath eastwards. Where this emerges by Court Farm continue past the attractive church and take the signposted public bridleway to the right, across fields. There is a junction of tracks at the top of Vann Hill, and you should turn right down the wide track that becomes the surfaced Upper Vann Lane. When it finally meets a road turn left along the drive to Burgate Farm, then right at the

signpost (bridlepath) until the surfaced track swings left into trees - and here carry straight on.

Turn right at a public footpath sign through a plantation called Standages. It crosses a couple of streams and passes some well-executed coppicing; and then via stiles through two fields (keep to the right-hand edge) it eventually hops on to the drive of Pear Tree Cottage and reaches a road. Here turn right, and shortly right again on to the drive to Field Place. (Continue

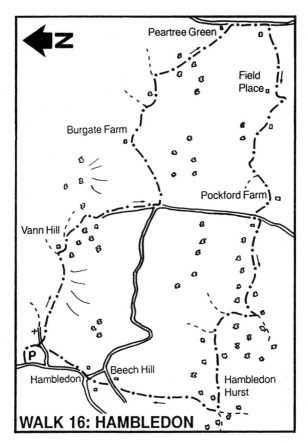

WALK 16: HAMBLEDON

along the road if you want to visit Dunsfold for refreshments.)

Nearing Field Place stay on the wide track as it curves down into a hollow then up to Duns Farm. Go through the gate in front of you, bordered by privet hedges, and past the farm to a gated bridleway in bushes ahead. Soon go through a gate on the right and around the upper edge of a sloping field (ignore the path down across the middle). At the far side go through one gate, then left through another, and follow the right edge of a field all the way to Pockford Farm and turn down its drive to the road.

Turn left on to the road then immediately right, and beyond a bungalow and double gates follow a rough track across meadows to woodland at the very far side. The path can now become a little muddy, as it sticks close to the bank of a stream. Where fencing begins on the right take the clear track uphill until it levels out, when you should take a fork left. There are many small paths through Hambledon Hurst, a beautiful area of ancient mixed wood-land, but essentially stay on the main track almost due west-wards, keeping some clearings you will glimpse to your right. After half a mile there is a cross-roads of bridleways, within sight of an untidy piece of waste land known as Cuckoo Corner. Turn right, and take a firmer and more direct track north, which once used to be the Godalming-Chiddingfold road. After a further half a mile go right through some wooden posts and down the drive of Philpotts Cottage. Cross a plank bridge on the right and follow the obvious path to the road.

The bridleway continues virtually opposite, and emerges by the lovely brick cottages of Beech Hill. Go forwards up the hill through Hambledon village, then via steps on the right by Matterves House which leads to a footpath across a wide field to St Peter's Church - and back down to the car park.

ALONG THE WAY:
Hambledon: The scattered village is full of lovely old buildings, many in local brick, and several with preservation orders. In the churchyard of St Peter's Church there is an old hollow yew where, it is claimed, up to 12 people can hide. To the south of the village Hambledon Hurst is a remnant of Weald Forest, once a vast spread of thick, mixed wood-land that spread across much of south Surrey and Sussex.

And finally, a celebratory orange squash in the garden of The Merry Harriers pub is recommended after complet-ing this walk. But don't take seriously the sign by the road outside: "Open for warm beer and lousy food"!

Tree care: Few, if any, of the woods in Surrey are completely wild and natural. Woodland management is taken seriously by large landowners like the National Trust, who often employ traditional practices such as selective felling - allowing more space and light for the stronger trees to grow - and coppicing (pruning the older trees).

WALK 17:
LEITH HILL

An interesting and invigorating walk that includes
the highest point in South East England, Leith Hill,
with views to match. After a descent to the village
of Coldharbour, long and quiet forest tracks lead
down to the young Tilling Bourne stream, then to
the picturesque hammer pond at Friday Street,
and via the broadleaves of Abinger Common back
to Holmbury.

Start: Holmbury St Mary. GR.110444.
Bus Routes 21, 433, 525, 588 (Guildford-Dorking).
Maps: OS Landranger 187/Pathfinder 1226.
Total distance: 12km (7½ miles).
Height gain: 355m (1165 feet).
Difficulty: Quite demanding, with plenty of ups and downs. Two of the
descents are particularly steep, and care must be exercised if the
ground is wet. Since many of the tracks are also used by
mountain bike riders, be alert.

THE WALK:
From the church at Holmbury St
Mary walk south along the
pavement and turn left just
after the garage on to the
Abinger Common/Leith Hill
road. At the first bend take the
bridleway off right, which then
climbs gradually up through
mixed woods. At High Ashes
Farm, from where there are the
first good views, continue along
the sandy track to a T-junction
and turn right. Very soon look
for a blue 'GW' (Greensand
Way) sign to a path half-left,
and at the far end of this, turn
left uphill to the road. Take the
wide, signposted path opposite
to the summit of Leith Hill, with
its elegant tower.

Once refreshed with both
views and food and drink, carry
on past the tower eastwards,

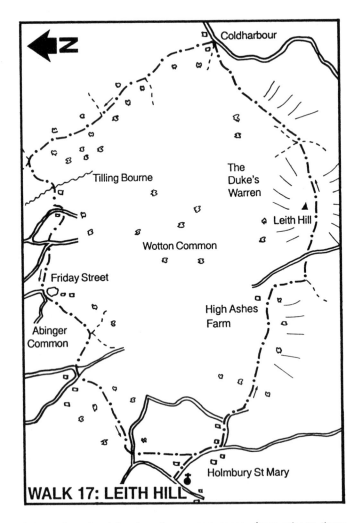

WALK 17: LEITH HILL

down a steep track to a junction of paths. Yours is half-right (NOT ahead into Dukes Warren) and out on to the top of the hillside once more, from where there are further panoramic views to Gatwick Airport and the Sussex Downs. Now follow the route of the National Trust Coldharbour Walk, indicated by small green waymarks. This follows a path off left into a coppice (do NOT take the main path downhill), then where it finishes turn left on to a wider track. Follow this level path across Coldharbour Common, and where the waymarks indicate left continue forwards until you meet a wide lane running down from the cricket pitch (in sight). Take this all the way down to Coldharbour village.

You emerge opposite The Plough, which boasts that it is the highest pub in South East England. Now turn sharp left along an unsurfaced lane past Crockers Wood Cottages towards the Forestry Commission's Buryhill Woods. At a sign which reads: 'Protect wildlife - please keep dogs on a lead' keep to the main track (half-left), and follow this public bridleway for over a mile. Ignore all turnings, go past the derelict Upper Merriden Farm and Tankards Pond, then take the middle of three tracks through a dense plantation of pines. At a crossroads of paths turn left, and soon a large, open nursery of young trees appears on your right. This path then drops steeply and crosses the infant, gurgling Tilling Bourne.

Now turn right on to a lane, then left on to a minor road by riding stables. Almost immediately turn right once more by a Wotton Parish Council noticeboard and up a narrow path, which swings right then veers left up a sunken corridor. The path crosses two roads, and continues straight on and down to Friday Street past the National Trust's Severell's Copse.

For relaxation there is a bench by the attractive pond, or the nearby Stephen Langton pub (named after the Archbishop of Canterbury born close to here who persuaded King John to sign the Magna Carta in 1215).

The pond was originally constructed to provide water power to drive the bellows and hammers used in the small but important local iron industry, and this and other artificially-constructed lakes were known as hammer ponds.

From the water follow the road west for a few yards, then left up a signposted sunken bridleway (ignore the steps to the right). The route is through the pine and birch woodland of Abinger Common, turning half-right at a 5-way junction of paths (follow the direction of the telephone wires overhead), then right at a crossroads of larger tracks. Emerge at a triangular green, with a well, and cross the two roads ahead for a path down beside Pasturewood Cottage. This path continues into woodland and develops into a wide forest drive. Carry on until the end, then carefully negotiate a very steep descent to the stile at the bottom; after which you should turn left and take a wide track behind gardens until it joins a lane that returns to the main road in Holmbury (turn right to finish at the church - or the pub).

ALONG THE WAY:

Leith Hill: At 295m, or 965 feet, this is the highest point in South East England. The tower was built in 1766 by local man Richard Hull, and in accordance with his wishes he was actually buried inside it. The folly adds enough extra height to bring the hill's overall figure to over 1000 feet and thus allow Leith Hill to be rather dubiously described as South East England's only mountain! The tower is open on weekends, April-September, and there is a small entrance fee. For this you get an exhibition and amazing views from the top - London, the Chilterns and the South Downs can all be visible on a clear day - but restrain those over-eager for a view from climbing the rather low parapets. Refreshments are also available.

Birdlife: The greensand hills of Surrey support considerable stands of lovely, mixed woodland, and this in turn supports a rich birdlife. The titmice family is one of the most common that you will see. They are small and acrobatic and often nest in holes in trees. Look out for the bright yellow and black coloured great tit (its song resembles "teacher, teacher"), and the distinctive long-tailed tit, which unlike the others nests in domes of bound lichen, moss and cobwebs that it suspends from branches and bushes. If you are quiet and observant you may also spot the uncommon stonechat, a small heathland bird with a black head and white patch on the side of the neck that has recently returned to Leith Hill. Its call sounds like two pebbles being banged together.